THE OLD BARN

SPRINGTIME

Joe Maniscalco

Ⴌ

REVIEW AND HERALD® PUBLISHING ASSOCIATION
WASHINGTON, DC 20039-0555
HAGERSTOWN, MD 21740

The author assumes full responsibility for the accuracy of all
facts and quotations as cited in this book.

This book was
Edited by Penny Estes Wheeler
Designed by Dennis Ferree
Cover art by Joe Maniscalco

Type set: Baskerville 12/14

PRINTED IN U.S.A.

R&H Cataloging Service

Maniscalco, Joe, 1926-
   The old barn: springtime.

   1. Spring—Pictorial works.
2. Spring—Juvenile literature.
I. Title.

                525.5

ISBN 0-8280-0423-4

Dedication

To our grandchildren—
Patrick
Brock
Savanna

Have you ever wondered what it would be like to live on a farm? Today most boys and girls live in the city. But many years ago most people lived in the country. They rode horses and rode in horse-drawn wagons instead of cars. They raised cows and chickens. Some kept goats and sheep, too, and almost everyone had dogs and cats. They had big gardens because they grew their own food. Mothers, aunts, and grandmas made everyone's clothes. Some even knew how to weave straw into hats. Everyone kept busy on a farm.

This is the story of the Hayden family. Daddy, Mother, 12-year-old Jim, 7-year-old Sunrise, and 5-year-old Gabriel. They had a dog named Patches and a cat named Fluffy, too.

The Haydens lived in north-eastern Washington state. The winters there were very long. Everybody was happy when springtime came. The wild flowers seemed to leap out of the earth. Their beautiful colors covered the countryside.

One day Gabriel and Sunrise were walking on the hills near their farm. As they walked along, they heard a faint honking sound. It grew louder and closer. They looked up, up, up and saw Canadian geese flying overhead. The geese, flying in an ever-moving "V," seemed to be talking to each other.

In the fall, Canadian geese fly south where it is warmer. Northern lakes freeze during the winter and this makes it harder for geese to find food. "You know that spring is coming when you see the geese flying northward," Sunrise told Gabriel.

"I wish I could fly like the geese," he said.

When the geese settle down after their long flight, they raise their families. Geese make their homes on the ground near water. Most geese build nests of twigs and grass, lining their nests with soft feathers. Father goose is called a gander. The mother is simply called a goose and baby geese are known as goslings.

Mother goose may lay as few as three eggs or as many as ten. Both mother and father look alike. Their heads and long necks look like they are covered with black stockings and they have white patches on their cheeks. The baby geese look like fluffy yellow balls. Mother and Father goose stay together for life. Geese live a long time for a bird. Some live thirty years or more.

Because there was so much to do on a farm, everyone in the Hayden family had a job. Sunrise took care of the calves. Calves grow fast and stay hungry most of the time. Their ears twitch all directions. They can hear almost anything.

Sunrise called her pet calf Big Eyes. Every time she brought food to Big Eyes, the calf sniffed with her moist nose.

Cows walk on two toes called split hoofs. Although calves have short legs, they are good runners. They can be good jumpers too. A cow at play is a funny sight. She lifts her tail straight up like a flag, kicks her legs, and almost looks like she's smiling. Unlike horses, cows do not lie flat on their sides when resting. A cow rests with her legs under her.

Sunrise liked to feed and brush Big Eyes. Animals understand kindness. Sunrise was always kind to her animals.

A barn would not be a barn without swallows. Like geese, swallows fly south in the winter. When springtime comes, they fly back north. Hundreds of swallows came to the Hayden farm each spring. Everyone was happy when they arrived for they ate lots of mosquitoes.

Swallows are fast flyers and their beaks are short and wide. Flying swiftly, they easily catch insects in their wide-open mouths. Swallows have short legs and small feet, and long, narrow wings. This is why they can fly so fast.

S wallows build cup-shaped nests of mud and grass in a barn. They line their nests with soft feathers. Sometimes the nests are so close to each other that the sides touch. Mother barn swallow lays from four to six eggs. The eggs are white with brown specks. After the eggs are hatched, the mother and father swallows feed the babies all day long. The parents keep on feeding them long after they leave the nest. The Hayden children laughed to see a line of young swallows sitting on a fence. The parents were still catching insects for their well-grown youngsters.

Now and then Gabriel would
climb into the barn and sit on the soft hay. He liked to watch the
swallows from inside the barn. He could see them fly to the
banks of a nearby creek. Scooping up mud in their beaks, they
would fly toward the barn. There were so many nests in the
barn that Gabriel wondered how the swallows could find their
own. But they never got mixed up. Gabriel thought the
swallows were wearing red-brown vests with blue coats on their
backs. Their forked tails looked like "coat tails." Gabriel could
enjoy watching the swallows for hours.

"Gabriel, where are you?" Mother called. "I need some more clean pails for the milking." After the cows were milked, Mother led them out into the pasture. There a brown cow could eat green grass so she could give white milk. Gabriel swept out the stalls after the cows left the barn. It was a hard job but it made him strong. Daddy put clean straw in each stall. In this way, the cows were kept clean and healthy. The Haydens sold the milk so they could make a little extra money. One of the main reasons for the Hayden barn was to make a home for the cows.

Sunrise thought that the sheep were some of the most interesting animals on the farm. She especially liked to feed the lambs. She knew when they were happy because they wagged their long tails. Young lambs have long legs. In just a few days after they are born, they can walk four or five miles following the other sheep. Sheep talk to each other by bleating. In this way, they know where each one is. When danger is near, they grow silent. Sheep can eat grass even when it is very short. They can cut grass off at its roots. When a sheep is angry, he stamps the ground with his front feet. Gabriel liked to watch the sheep too. But most of all he liked to watch the lambs.

Two baby kids were born in the spring. Gabriel liked to be with the baby goats. They sniffed him and chewed on his clothes but he just laughed.

Goats are good runners and jumpers. When angry, the goat shakes his head. When frightened, it lowers its head and butts. Goats are good climbers. They will climb to the top of a building if they can. Baby goats make good pets. The two kids followed Gabriel everywhere he went.

Sunrise and Gabriel had a
horse named Sherry Dell. She was a small horse, or a pony.

When Daddy brought home Sherry Dell, he told the children to take good care of her. They loved her. In the wintertime, they made sure she had plenty of hay. Sometimes Sherry Dell walked down to the creek to drink. Gabriel liked to hold the reins while Sunrise brushed the pony. When the flies bothered her, she'd brush them off by flipping her long tail. As a special treat, Gabriel and Sunrise would bring Sherry Dell a nice red apple or a bucket of oats.

The old barn had all kinds of creatures living in it. Mice liked the grain and made their nests under the hay. Ground squirrels and chipmunks liked the grain too.

A night-flying creature also lived in the barn. It was the bat. Although the bat's wings are different from those of birds, they are good fliers. Just as the sun is setting bats fly out of the barn, their mouths open. In this way they catch many insects. The bat's voice sounds like the squeak of a toy wheelbarrow.

A skunk family also lived under the barn near some ground squirrels. Skunks move slowly for they don't need to run fast. When something bothers them, they lift up their tails and spray! It smells awful.

Sunrise and Gabriel often played near the barn. The hay was soft. They would climb up a platform and jump into the soft hay. It was fun. Before winter came, all the hay had to be put in the barn. Inside the barn, it would stay dry when rain or snow covered the ground. Grass does not grow tall in the winter so the animals must eat hay that was cut during the hot summer time. Wet hay will rot and would make the animals sick.

So the Haydens always kept dry hay in the barn.

There are probably more mice on a farm than any other animals. Mice like a barn because it is so full of good food. They like to nibble at the bin of oats stored there. Many animals like oats. Oats keep them healthy. Even people eat oats. The Hayden family often ate oatmeal for breakfast.

Have you ever wondered why a mouse has such a long tail? He uses his tail to help him when he climbs. It also helps him when he jumps. Mice like to run along a wall with their whiskers touching the wall. This helps to guide them. A mouse's hind legs are longer and stronger than the front legs so he's a good jumper. Mice eat almost anything that people eat. They like fruit and vegetables. When eating, mice hold their food in their front paws like a squirrel. Mice have big ears and can hear the slightest sound. Mice must be very careful in a barn because so many other creatures would like to eat them.

Have you ever heard of the barn owl? Barn owls like to nest in a barn. This owl has long legs, strong claws, and a heart-shaped face. An owl makes no noise when it flies, for the feathers on its wings are soft. Barn owls can swoop down on a mouse and grab him before he knows what happened. Their big yellow eyes see well at night and they like to sleep during the day.

Mother owl lays five to seven white eggs. She takes good care of them and of her babies. Sometimes the barn owl is called the "monkey-faced owl." Do you think his face looks something like a monkey's face? The brown color of the owl makes it hard to see during the day when it is high up in the barn. Many other kinds of owls lived around the old barn too. And they all liked to eat mice.

Springtime is the
time for putting in a garden and the Hayden family
planted all kinds of seeds. They planted radish seeds and
carrot seeds. They planted corn and lettuce, onions and pota-
toes. The soil had to be worked with a hoe and all the
weeds had to be pulled. All the Haydens thought gardening
was fun. They knew the exercise was good for them, too.
Sometimes as they worked, they saw robins flying
northward. Sunrise and Gabriel liked to watch the
robins. The fat little birds with orange breasts
seemed to be everywhere. The children
watched the robins hopping about
their garden.

As the robins hopped in the garden, they stopped now and then, listening. A robin's head would cock to the side. Then his head would bob down and he'd snatch up a worm.

Robins make their nests of mud and grass. Mother robin lays four blue eggs. In about two weeks the eggs hatch and four baby robins need to be fed. This is one reason the robins catch so many worms.

Like the robins, the pretty yellow dandelions seem to be everywhere in the spring. New dandelion leaves are good to eat. The Hayden family liked to eat cooked dandelion greens.

As the week days passed, many chores had to be finished. The stalls in the barn were cleaned. The animals were fed. There are many gates and fences on a farm. These keep the horses and cows in their pastures. If a gate is left open, they are sure to get out. Once a horse or cow gets out of its pasture, it may roam for miles.

The grass always looks better on the other side of the fence, so Gabriel and Sunrise made sure that the gates were kept closed. Sometimes the gates were hard to close so they had to help each other. Even Patches tried to help close the gates.

In the spring, one of the farm horses had a baby horse. Baby horses are called colts. Colts are fun to watch. They have long legs, short tails, and are good runners, too. Springtime was the best time of the year for farm animals. The new grass was tender and tasted good. After the long winter the warmer weather felt good too.

As the sun was ready to set on a Friday afternoon, the Hayden family were all home. Everyone had bathed and was dressed in clean clothes. All the animals were fed and put to bed, and all the gates were closed. This was a special time because the Sabbath was about to begin. The Bible says, "Remember the sabbath day to keep it holy."

As the sun dropped in the west, our farm family sang songs about Jesus. This was worship time. As they sang inside the house they could hear singing outside. Coyotes roamed around the farm and they howled almost every night. Coyotes look like a medium-sized dog with a long pointed nose and bushy tail. Gabriel and Sunrise and Jim were happy that the Sabbath came every week. The family could rest from work and enjoy the Lord's day.

S abbath is a time for church. The Hayden family liked to go to church and study the Bible. After church they went home and ate the special dinner Mother had planned. Sometimes they walked up the creek in the afternoon. Once in a while they would see a beaver swim in the creek. If they were quiet, the beaver might climb up the bank and eat the dandelions. The children liked nature walks on Sabbath. There was so much to see.

Old barns are a lot of fun. If the old barn could talk, it would tell you of all the creatures that go in and out. It would tell you about the creatures it could see from its windows.

Birds like the eagle, the osprey, and the kingfisher that catches fish in the creek might be seen from its windows. Deer come to the creek to drink now and then. Once in a while a bear comes, too. There are porcupines and raccoons and all sorts of animals to see. Yes, the old barn is an interesting place. Don't you think so?